Psychology and Christian Faith

Adrian Collins

Adrian Collins

Copyright Page

Adrian Collins

4

Index

Adrian Collins

An Unexpected Encounter

Psychology and the Christian faith seem, at first glance, to be two completely separate fields. On the one hand, psychology presents itself as a science that studies human behavior, the mind, and emotions from an objective, evidence-based perspective. On the other hand, the Christian faith focuses on spirituality, on the belief in God and the teachings of Jesus, promoting values and practices that seek the salvation of the soul. However, if we look deeper, we can find that both paths, although different, have something in common: both seek to understand and improve human life.

Throughout history, these two fields have met more frequently than one might think. For centuries, the Christian religion was one of the main sources of comfort for people suffering from emotional or mental problems. In times when psychology did not yet exist as a science, people turned to the church and their faith to find answers about the meaning of their suffering, their anxieties and their inner doubts. Prayer, confession and the advice of religious leaders were the tools used to deal with emotional difficulties. In many cases, these practices brought relief to people, as they felt they were receiving both spiritual and emotional support.

However, with the emergence of psychology as a science, a division began to emerge. Psychology attempted to explain emotional and mental phenomena through theories and studies, while religion continued to offer a vision based on faith and the spiritual. Many psychologists in their early years of study were skeptical of the idea of including religion as part of the understanding of human behavior. For some, religion was seen as a source of repression or as a form of control over the masses. The church, on the other hand, viewed psychology with suspicion, considering it a threat to its beliefs, as it seemed to divert attention from the divine to more earthly and scientific explanations.

Despite these differences, what many fail to consider is that the Christian faith and psychology do not necessarily have to be in conflict. The two disciplines can complement each other in interesting ways. The Christian faith, with its emphasis on love, forgiveness, compassion, and hope, provides values and teachings that have a profound impact on the human mind. Psychology, on the other hand, helps us understand how these beliefs influence behavior, emotions, and the way people deal with life's challenges.

For example, studies have shown that people who have a strong faith in something, whether it be a religion or a spiritual purpose, tend to have greater resilience in the face of stress and adversity. Faith provides a frame of reference that makes sense of difficulties. For believers, times of suffering can be seen as tests or lessons that God puts in their path so that they can grow as individuals. This approach helps many people overcome hopelessness, find strength where they didn't have it before, and maintain a positive attitude even in difficult times.

Psychology has also begun to recognize the importance of spirituality in mental health.

Not all emotional problems are resolved with therapy or medication; often, people need something deeper to help them find inner peace. Spirituality offers a connection to something larger than oneself, which for many people is a source of comfort. By integrating spiritual elements into psychotherapy, some practitioners have found that their patients experience more significant and lasting improvements in their emotional well-being.

On the other hand, the Christian faith can also benefit from psychology. Understanding how human emotions work, how to deal with stress, and how to overcome trauma are valuable insights that religious leaders can incorporate into their pastoral guidance. Emotional well-being is not something that should be ignored in spiritual life. Believers are also human beings with psychological needs, and the church, by integrating some concepts from psychology, can provide more comprehensive support to its followers. Priests, pastors, and leaders can learn to recognize signs of depression, anxiety, or stress in their parishioners, and instead of only offering spiritual answers, they can also guide them toward professional support when needed.

What is interesting is that, even though these fields initially seemed to be in conflict, more and more psychologists and religious leaders are finding ways to collaborate and enrich each other. Psychology does not try to replace faith, and faith should not try to negate the importance of science. On the contrary, when they are combined appropriately, they can offer more complete solutions to the problems people face in their daily lives.

In short, this "unexpected encounter" between psychology and the Christian faith is far from being a confrontation. It is rather an opportunity for both fields to work together and find ways to improve people's well-being on all levels: mental, emotional and spiritual. Although each has its own approach, the ultimate goal is the same: to help people live a fuller, more balanced life, at peace with themselves and the world around them.

The Power of Faith in the Human Mind

Faith is a powerful element in the lives of many people. No matter what the specific belief is, whether it is faith in God, in a higher being, in a greater purpose, or in the power of good, the fact is that faith has a profound impact on the human mind. When we talk about the Christian faith, we are referring to an absolute trust in the existence of God, in His promises, and in the belief that through Him, people can find meaning and purpose in life. This conviction not only affects what a person believes, but also how he or she thinks, how he or she acts, and how he or she faces life's challenges.

The human mind is incredibly complex, and faith works on many levels within it. One of the most notable effects of faith on the human mind is its ability to provide comfort in times of distress. When people face difficult situations such as the loss of a loved one, illness, poverty, or suffering, faith offers a source of hope that enables them to carry on. Belief that God has a plan, or that everything happens for a reason, provides a perspective that makes problems seem more manageable. Faith helps people not feel alone in their grief, but rather see themselves as part of something larger than themselves.

This power of faith is more than just emotional comfort. Psychological studies have shown that people with strong faith tend to have lower levels of stress and anxiety. This is partly because faith acts as an emotional anchor. People who believe in a divine purpose for their lives, or in guidance from a higher being, tend to face challenges with more calm and determination. They have the certainty that even if they don't fully understand what's happening, God is in control. This reduces the fear of the unknown, which is one of the main sources of anxiety in human beings. Instead of feeling trapped or hopeless, believers find in their faith the strength to keep going.

Another important aspect of the power of faith on the human mind is its ability to transform the way people perceive their problems. For someone with Christian faith, life's difficulties are not simply obstacles or punishments, but rather opportunities to grow spiritually. This mindset completely changes the way they deal with pain and suffering. Instead of seeing adversity as something negative, faith allows them to see suffering as a test or as a means to reach a greater understanding or connection with God. This positive outlook helps them maintain a resilient attitude, even in the darkest of times.

Faith also influences how people view their own worth. In the Christian faith, each individual is seen as a creation of God, loved and valuable in His eyes. This belief that one is important to a higher being has a profound impact on self-esteem and self-worth. People who feel they have a God-given purpose tend to experience a greater sense of personal value. This sense of purpose is critical to mental health, as it provides a reason to live, a reason to fight, and a reason to be a better person every day. No matter how tough the circumstances, faith provides a sense that life has meaning, and this is a fundamental pillar to maintaining a healthy mind.

Furthermore, faith promotes behaviors that are beneficial to the mind and emotional well-being. In most Christian teachings, love, forgiveness, compassion, and service to others are promoted. These values not only help improve interpersonal relationships, but also have a positive impact on the mental health of those who practice them. People who live according to these principles tend to experience less resentment, less anger, and less envy, which contributes to a calmer and more balanced mind. The act of forgiveness, for example, frees the mind from the emotional burden of hatred and resentment, allowing the person to feel freer and more at peace with themselves.

Prayer, one of the most common practices within Christianity, also has positive effects on the human mind. Not only is prayer a way to communicate with God, but it also acts as a method of meditation and reflection. Through prayer, people can calm their mind, focus on what is important, and release the tensions and worries of the day. In fact, many studies have shown that the regular practice of prayer or meditation can reduce stress levels and improve concentration and mental clarity. Furthermore, the feeling of being in touch with something greater than oneself, through prayer, provides an inner peace that is difficult to find in other aspects of life.

Another significant impact of faith on the human mind is the ability to create a supportive community. For many believers, the church is not only a place of worship, but also a place of social connection. People who share a common faith tend to form strong bonds and support each other in times of need. This support network is critical to mental health, as it provides a sense of belonging and solidarity. People who feel connected to a religious community often experience fewer feelings of loneliness and isolation, which contributes to better emotional health.

In short, the power of faith on the human mind is vast and profound. It is not just abstract beliefs or religious rituals, but a force that shapes the way people think, feel, and act. Faith provides a sense of purpose, a source of comfort in difficult times, and a guide to living a more compassionate and loving life. It is a powerful tool for mental well-being, and while it does not completely eliminate life's problems, it does offer a way to face them with more hope and strength. Faith, in essence, transforms the human mind by offering a vision of the world where, despite difficulties, there is always light and hope.

Religious Beliefs and Identity Development

Religious beliefs play a fundamental role in the development of a person's identity, especially when these beliefs are introduced from an early age. Identity is not something that is formed overnight, it is the result of years of experiences, influences, and decisions that accumulate throughout life. And when we talk about religion, especially in the context of Christianity, we are talking about a set of beliefs, values, and teachings that can shape the way a person views themselves and the world around them.

When a person grows up in a religious environment, such as a devout Christian family, it is very likely that their sense of who they are and what they stand for is deeply influenced by those beliefs. From childhood, they are taught certain principles: that God is the creator of everything, that they have a divine purpose in their life, that they should follow the commandments and live according to the teachings of Jesus. These concepts not only shape behavior, but also the way a person perceives themselves. From a very young age, they may begin to see themselves as someone special in God's eyes, as someone who has a greater purpose in this world. This sense of purpose is something that, throughout life, reinforces a person's identity.

Identity development is directly related to the experiences and responses that an individual gets from the world around him or her. Religious beliefs provide a framework through which a person can interpret his or her experiences. For example, a child who faces a challenge in life, such as an illness or a difficulty at school, may interpret this challenge through the religious teachings he or she has received. Instead of seeing it as a mere obstacle, he or she might see it as a test of faith, as something that God has put in his or her path to strengthen him or her. This way of interpreting experiences not only affects how he or she deals with the problem at hand, but also how he or she sees himself or herself as a "child of God" who has the strength to overcome difficulties.

Furthermore, religious beliefs not only influence how a person views the world, but also how they interact with others. In Christianity, values such as humility, charity, love of neighbor, and forgiveness are promoted. These values are not just abstract ideas; they are practical guides that shape daily behavior and, in turn, reinforce a person's identity. If someone grows up believing that they should forgive those who have hurt them or that they should love others regardless of differences, those acts not only become part of their daily routine, but also part of their identity. They begin to see themselves as someone who is kind, who is compassionate, and who always looks for the good in others, which reinforces their sense of who they are in the world.

Another important aspect is how religious beliefs can provide a sense of belonging. Being part of a religious community, such as a church, gives a person a reference group with which they can identify. This sense of belonging is crucial in the development of identity, as people, especially young people, constantly seek out groups they can join in order to feel accepted and understood. By being part of a Christian community, a person not only adopts the beliefs of that community, but also finds support, understanding, and a place where their identity is validated. This sense of belonging reinforces identity by giving a person a context in which they can define themselves.

However, the impact of religious beliefs on identity development is not always positive or straightforward. In some cases, religious teachings may conflict with other aspects of a person's life, which can lead to confusion or internal tension. For example, someone who grows up in a very conservative Christian home might have difficulty accepting certain aspects of their personal identity, such as their sexual orientation or career interests, if they feel that they do not fit with the religious expectations that have been instilled in them. This internal conflict can lead to an identity crisis, in which the person struggles to reconcile their religious beliefs with their true self. In these cases, the process of identity development can be more complicated and painful, as the person feels that they must choose between being true to their religious beliefs or being true to themselves.

In addition, in some religious contexts, beliefs can be very rigid, which can limit a person's freedom to explore different aspects of their identity. Some Christian teachings can be very strict about what is considered acceptable in terms of behaviour and thinking. This can lead to a person repressing certain aspects of themselves, which can affect their emotional well-being and personal development. In these cases, religion can become a source of internal tension, as the person feels they must fit into a pre-established mould, rather than freely exploring who they are.

On the other hand, there are many people who find that their faith provides them with a solid foundation to explore their identity more deeply. Christianity teaches that each person is unique and has a God-given purpose. This idea can be tremendously empowering, as it gives a person the freedom to explore their gifts, talents, and place in the world, knowing that, in the end, it is all part of a divine plan. For many, this belief provides a firm foundation from which they can develop a strong and secure identity.

In summary, religious beliefs play a key role in the development of a person's identity. They provide a frame of reference, a sense of purpose and belonging, and guide behavior and interactions with others. However, the impact of religious beliefs on identity is not always uniform; it can be a source of strength, but it can also generate internal conflict. Ultimately, how religious beliefs affect identity development depends largely on how those beliefs are interpreted and applied in daily life.

The Role of the Christian Community in Mental Health

The Christian community plays a very important role in the mental health of the people who are part of it. The idea of living in community is not just a social concept, but is deeply rooted in Christian principles. Since the time of Jesus, community life has been seen as a form of mutual support, love and compassion among believers. Today, belonging to a Christian community can offer much more than just a space to practice faith; it can also be a significant source of emotional and mental well-being.

One of the most obvious benefits of being part of a Christian community is the sense of belonging. We all need to feel part of something bigger, to be accepted and valued for who we are. In a Christian community, people have the opportunity to connect with others who share their beliefs and values, which creates an accepting and supportive environment. This sense of belonging is vital for mental health, as it reduces feelings of loneliness and isolation, which are two of the biggest contributors to problems like depression and anxiety.

In addition, the Christian community provides a very strong emotional support system. When a person is facing difficulties in life, such as the loss of a loved one, financial problems, or family conflicts, the community is there to offer comfort and help. Simply knowing that there are people willing to listen, pray together, and offer words of encouragement can make a huge difference in how someone copes with their problems. This support is not only emotional, but also practical. In many Christian communities, it is common for members to help each other in concrete ways, whether it is offering material help, food, or even financial assistance. This type of help reinforces the sense that we are not alone in our struggles, which is essential to maintaining a healthy mind.

Another important aspect is the role of shared faith. Faith in God and in the principles of Christianity provides a framework for understanding life's challenges. In a Christian community, people share not only their problems, but also their faith that God has a plan and that there is hope even in the darkest of times. This perspective can be very comforting, as it provides a sense of purpose and direction, helping people to maintain a positive and resilient attitude in the face of difficulties. Believing that there is a greater purpose, even in suffering, allows people to view problems in a more hopeful light, which alleviates stress and mental anguish.

Group prayer also plays an important role in emotional and mental well-being within the Christian community. When people pray together, they are not only expressing their faith, but they are also connecting in a deep way with others. Communal prayer can create an environment of peace and calm, which helps reduce anxiety and foster a sense of unity. Additionally, praying for others and knowing that others are praying for you creates a sense of spiritual support, which is very powerful for mental well-being. This collective spiritual connection has a therapeutic effect that goes beyond words; it is an experience of inner peace that many people describe as healing.

The Christian community also promotes values that are beneficial for mental health, such as forgiveness, empathy, and compassion. These values not only improve relationships between people, but also help release negative emotions that can affect mental health. Forgiveness, for example, is a key principle in Christianity, and practicing it can ease the emotional burden of anger, resentment, and hatred. By letting go of those negative emotions, the mind is freed from unnecessary tension, allowing for greater emotional well-being. Empathy and compassion, meanwhile, foster an environment in which people feel understood and valued, reducing feelings of isolation and loneliness.

In addition, the Christian community provides a space for reflection and personal growth. Through sermons, Bible studies, and other religious activities, community members have the opportunity to explore deeper aspects of their lives and faith. These moments of reflection can be very beneficial for mental health, as they allow people to analyze their emotions, thoughts, and behaviors in light of their beliefs. By doing so, they can find new ways to deal with problems and develop greater emotional and spiritual strength.

A less talked about but equally important aspect is how Christian community can provide structure and a sense of routine that is critical to mental well-being. Attending church regularly, participating in prayer groups or Bible studies, and being involved in community activities offers structure that gives stability to a person's life. This routine can be particularly helpful in times of crisis or instability, as it provides a sense of normalcy and continuity. Knowing that each week there is a place where one can go to find peace, support, and community can be a source of comfort and security for many people.

It is important to mention that in many cases, Christian communities also provide access to additional resources for emotional and psychological support. In some churches, there are counselors or pastors who are trained in offering spiritual guidance that is also aligned with basic psychological principles. These spiritual leaders can offer a combination of emotional support and faith-based advice that helps people better manage their emotions and mental issues. In some cases, churches even organize support groups for people dealing with specific issues such as grief, depression, or addictions, which can be a valuable resource for those seeking help within a Christian context.

Of course, it's important to remember that not all experiences within a Christian community are perfect. Sometimes, people may face judgment or feel excluded if they don't completely fit in with the community's norms or expectations. These challenges can also take a toll on mental health, especially if a person feels like they aren't living up to religious expectations or aren't "good" enough as a Christian. However, many modern Christian communities are working to be more inclusive and understanding, recognizing that everyone has struggles and that love and compassion are the most important principles.

In conclusion, the Christian community offers an environment that can be extremely beneficial for mental health. Through a sense of belonging, emotional support, shared faith, group prayer, and the promotion of positive values, people can find a refuge in their community from facing life's difficulties. The community provides a space where people can be heard, valued, and supported, which is essential for emotional and mental well-being. Although it does not completely eliminate problems, the Christian community offers tools and resources that help people face them with more hope, faith, and strength.

Guilt and Sin

Guilt and sin are two concepts deeply intertwined in Christian life, and have influenced the human mind since time immemorial. In Christianity, sin is understood as any action, thought, or behavior that goes against the will of God. That is, everything that is considered morally wrong according to the commandments and teachings of the Bible. Guilt, on the other hand, is the emotion that arises when a person recognizes that he or she has committed a sin. Although guilt is a common experience for many people, its impact on mental and emotional health can be very deep and often complex.

For many believers, sin is presented as some sort of standard or rule to be met. When a person fails to meet those standards, he or she feels guilty. This guilt can be a constant reminder that one has failed, both God and oneself. In that sense, guilt is not simply a passing feeling, but an emotional burden that many people carry around for years. It is important to understand that guilt, in the Christian context, arises not only from serious actions like lying or stealing, but also from more everyday things, like having impure thoughts, feeling envious, or not being generous enough. Thus, a person can find themselves trapped in a cycle of constantly feeling guilty, even about small things.

Guilt has a positive side in the spiritual life, as it can serve as a kind of internal alarm that indicates when a person has strayed from his or her path. In that sense, guilt can lead to repentance, which is an essential step in Christianity to restore one's relationship with God. Repentance is not only an acknowledgement of sin, but also a sincere commitment to change and do things differently. Many people find in this process of repentance a kind of emotional release, as they feel relieved to confess their mistakes and ask for forgiveness. On a psychological level, this act of confessing can have therapeutic effects, as it allows the person to release repressed emotions and, in turn, feel emotionally lighter.

However, not all experiences of guilt lead to a positive outcome. In some cases, guilt can become overwhelming, affecting self-esteem and mental well-being. Some people experience what is known as excessive or toxic guilt, a feeling that is disproportionate to the sin committed. For example, someone might constantly feel guilty about things that are not really under their control, such as involuntary thoughts or natural human desires. This type of guilt can lead to a cycle of harsh self-criticism, where the person judges themselves harshly and sees themselves as a bad person, which affects their mental health. In these cases, guilt ceases to be a corrective mechanism and becomes an emotional burden that prevents the person from advancing spiritually and living a full life.

In Christianity, it is taught that all human beings are sinners by nature. Ever since the original sin of Adam and Eve, humanity has been seen as imperfect and prone to making mistakes. This idea can create a sense of helplessness in some people, as they feel that no matter what they do, they will always be falling into sin. This concept, while theologically important, can be difficult to deal with from an emotional standpoint. If a person sees themselves as someone who is constantly failing and unable to achieve the perfection that God requires, they may experience feelings of hopelessness and frustration. This state of mind can lead to depression, as the person feels that there is no way out of their situation.

On the other hand, guilt can also be used as a tool of control within certain religious communities. In some contexts, sin and guilt are so emphasized that people begin to live in a constant state of fear of making a mistake or displeasing God. This type of teaching can lead to a form of manipulation, where religious leaders use guilt to keep people under control. For example, some leaders might teach that only through strict obedience to church rules can salvation be found, which puts enormous pressure on believers. This pressure can cause anxiety and stress, as people feel constantly watched and evaluated, not only by God, but also by the religious community.

It is important to mention that while sin and guilt are important themes in Christianity, so is the idea of forgiveness. Jesus taught that God is merciful and willing to forgive the sins of those who sincerely repent. This teaching is crucial to understanding the balance between sin, guilt, and mental health. While it is natural to feel guilty after making a mistake, Christianity offers a path to overcome that guilt through divine forgiveness. Knowing that God is willing to forgive can be an immense source of peace and comfort for many people. On a psychological level, this knowledge can help ease the emotional burden of guilt and allow a person to feel free to move forward.

However, not all people find it easy to accept forgiveness. Some people get stuck in guilt, unable to forgive themselves, even if they believe God has already forgiven them. This kind of internal conflict can be damaging to mental health, as the person continues to carry the burden of sin long after they have been forgiven. In these cases, it is important for people to learn to accept both God's forgiveness and forgiveness of themselves.

This is not always easy, as it involves a profound change in the way one sees oneself. Letting go of guilt does not mean ignoring sin, but recognizing that even though a mistake has been made, there is room for growth, healing, and reconciliation.

In the Christian life, guilt can also have an impact on interpersonal relationships. When a person feels that they have sinned, they may not only feel that they have failed God, but also others. For example, someone who has lied to or betrayed a friend may experience deep guilt, which can affect their ability to relate to that person in the future. Guilt can create emotional distance, as the person feels unworthy or ashamed. In these cases, the process of asking for forgiveness and seeking reconciliation is not only important for the relationship with God, but also for the restoration of human relationships. The Bible speaks of the importance of forgiving and being forgiven, which also has an impact on people's mental and emotional health. The act of asking for forgiveness and being forgiven by others can alleviate the emotional weight that guilt brings with it.

In short, guilt and sin are central themes in Christianity, and they have a significant impact on the human mind and emotions. While guilt can serve as a tool to correct behavior and seek repentance, it can also become an emotional burden if it becomes excessive or disproportionate. It is important for people to find a healthy balance between acknowledging their mistakes and accepting God's forgiveness. Likewise, it is crucial that guilt not be used as a tool of manipulation or control within religious communities, as this can negatively affect the mental health of believers. In the end, the Christian message of forgiveness and redemption offers a way out of guilt and an opportunity to live a full life, free from the burdens of the past.

The Power of Forgiveness

Forgiveness is one of the most powerful concepts within Christianity, and its impact goes far beyond the spiritual realm. The power of forgiveness has profound implications for people's emotional, mental, and relational lives. Forgiveness is not only an act of kindness toward others, but also a gift we give to ourselves. In this chapter, we will explore how forgiveness transforms lives, frees the heart from the burden of resentment, and helps us heal on both an emotional and spiritual level.

In Christianity, forgiveness is one of Jesus' most important teachings. In his words, we are to forgive not just once, but seventy times seven, implying that the act of forgiving must be ongoing and unconditional. This is because forgiveness not only benefits the person being forgiven, but it also frees the forgiver. When we carry resentment and anger for the harm done to us, we are actually imprisoning ourselves. These negative feelings take up space in our minds and hearts, creating a barrier that prevents us from experiencing peace and well-being.

One of the most powerful effects of forgiveness is the emotional release it produces. When someone has hurt us, it is natural to feel anger, hurt, or even hate. These feelings, although understandable, can become an emotional burden if they are held over time. Holding a grudge is like carrying a backpack full of stones; over time, that load becomes unbearable and prevents us from moving forward. Forgiving is like letting go of those stones, releasing that burden we carry and allowing us to move forward without that emotional weight. The moment we decide to forgive, we are not saying that what happened was right, nor are we justifying the behavior of the person who hurt us. Forgiving means that we have decided to let go of that pain in order to heal and find peace.

In addition to emotional release, forgiveness has a significant impact on our mental health. Resentment and bitterness can cause stress, anxiety, and depression. When we allow these feelings to build up, we are affecting our emotional well-being. Science also supports this concept; psychological studies have shown that people who practice forgiveness have lower stress levels and greater life satisfaction. This is because forgiveness allows us to stop reliving the past and helps us focus on the present, rather than getting stuck in the cycle of remembering pain and injustice.

The power of forgiveness also lies in its ability to heal relationships. In our lives, it is inevitable that at some point we will hurt others or be hurt. Human relationships are full of imperfections and misunderstandings, and conflict is a natural part of any relationship. However, the key to maintaining healthy relationships is not in avoiding conflict, but in knowing how to manage it and, when necessary, to forgive. Forgiving someone who has hurt us not only repairs the relationship, but also strengthens the bonds between people. In many cases, relationships become stronger after forgiveness has been granted, as both parties have learned to move past the conflict with compassion and understanding.

It is important to note that forgiveness does not always happen immediately, and it is not always easy. Forgiveness is a process, and sometimes it can take time. There are deep wounds that require gradual healing before the person is ready to forgive. This process may involve reflecting on the pain, talking about the experience with someone you trust, or even seeking professional help to deal with the trauma. The important thing to understand is that forgiveness is not an instant act, but a decision that is made over time and with the intention of freeing yourself from the past. Forgiveness is not forgetting, but remembering without feeling the pain that once affected us.

In the Christian context, forgiveness has an even deeper meaning. It is taught that we should forgive because God has forgiven us. According to the Christian faith, we are all sinners, and God in his mercy offers us forgiveness despite our faults. This act of love and grace is the foundation of Christianity, and believers are called to imitate that divine mercy in their own lives. When we forgive others, we are following God's example and showing the same love and compassion that He has shown us. This act of forgiveness is not only beneficial for our emotional and mental health, but it also brings us closer to God and to the principles of the faith.

One of the reasons some people find it difficult to forgive is the fear of appearing weak or vulnerable. Often, pride stops us from taking that step toward forgiveness, as we believe that by forgiving we are accepting that the other person "won" or that we are letting go of our own dignity. However, the true power of forgiveness is not in weakness, but in strength. Forgiveness requires great courage, because it means letting go of the control we think we have over the situation. When we forgive, we are saying that we will not allow the pain or injustice to define us. Instead of holding on to the hurt, we choose to move forward with compassion and understanding. This act of courage is what truly demonstrates strength of character.

Another aspect of forgiveness that is not always discussed is the importance of forgiving oneself. Often, we are able to forgive others, but we find it much more difficult to forgive ourselves for our own mistakes. Carrying around guilt and self-criticism can be one of the heaviest burdens we carry. Forgiveness of oneself is essential for inner peace. Christianity teaches that God has already forgiven us, and if He, in His infinite mercy, grants us forgiveness, why shouldn't we do so as well? Forgiving oneself is recognizing that we are human, that we make mistakes, but that those mistakes do not define who we are. It allows us to free ourselves from excessive self-demands and gives us the space to grow and improve.

Finally, forgiveness has the power to transform not only our individual lives, but also the world around us. When we choose to forgive, we are contributing to a more compassionate and peaceful environment. Resentment and unforgiveness are causes of many conflicts, both on a personal and societal level. Imagine a world where more people practice forgiveness, where instead of responding to hate with hate, the path of reconciliation is chosen. Although forgiveness does not always change external circumstances, it has the power to change our hearts and, in turn, the way we interact with others. When we forgive, we create space for peace and healing, not only in our lives, but in the lives of those around us.

In short, the power of forgiveness is immense. It frees us from the weight of resentment, improves our mental health, heals our relationships, and brings us closer to God. Although forgiveness is not always easy, it is an essential tool for living a full and peaceful life. By forgiving, we are not only benefiting the person who hurt us, but we are also healing our own hearts. In the end, forgiveness is an act of love: love toward others and love toward ourselves. It is an act that allows us to let go of the past and walk toward a future filled with peace, compassion, and understanding.

Faith and Anxiety

The relationship between faith and anxiety is a topic that has been explored by many people, especially those who seek relief in their faith when facing difficult times. Anxiety is an emotion that we all experience at some point in our lives. It is that feeling of worry or fear that overwhelms us when we think about the future, about everyday problems or about situations that are beyond our control. It can occur in a mild form, such as nervousness before an exam or an interview, or in a more intense form, causing deep discomfort that affects our mental and physical health. In this context, the Christian faith can play a fundamental role in managing that anxiety and helping us find peace in the midst of chaos.

Faith, at its core, is trust in something bigger than ourselves. For Christians, that trust is in God. When we face anxious times, our minds tend to focus on everything that could go wrong—worst-case scenarios. Faith, however, invites us to shift our perspective. Instead of focusing on our worries and fears, we are encouraged to trust that God has a plan, even when we can't see the full picture.

This trust doesn't mean our problems will magically disappear, but that we can stop fighting constant fear of the future and rest in the certainty that we are not alone in our struggles.

One of the most well-known passages in the Bible about anxiety is found in the Gospel of Matthew, where Jesus says: "Do not worry about tomorrow, for tomorrow will worry about itself." This teaching reminds us that worrying about what might happen in the future is, in a way, a waste of energy. It invites us to focus on the present, on the here and now, and to trust that God will guide us step by step. This is one of the most powerful aspects of faith: it gives us a sense of relief in the face of the unknown. While anxiety pushes us to live constantly in the future, faith calls us to live in the present with confidence and serenity.

Another important aspect is prayer. For many people, prayer is a way to connect with God, but it is also a powerful tool to calm the anxious mind. When we are overwhelmed by stress or uncertainty, prayer allows us to express our worries, release those burdens, and give them to God. Instead of trying to carry everything ourselves, prayer is a way to say, "God, I can't do this alone, I need your help." This practice can have a deeply calming effect on our minds. By verbalizing our fears and worries, we stop turning them over and over in our heads, and that gives us a respite, a sense of relief.

Faith also gives us a supportive community. Often times, people who experience anxiety feel isolated, as if they are the only ones struggling. However, the church and Christian community offer a space where those emotional burdens can be shared. Talking with other people of faith, hearing about their experiences, receiving words of encouragement, or simply knowing that there are people who are willing to pray for you can be a great comfort. Anxiety often makes us feel alone, but faith reminds us that we are not facing our difficulties alone, that we are part of a larger body that is there to support us.

It's important to recognize that while faith can be an invaluable resource for managing anxiety, this doesn't mean that people who suffer from severe anxiety must simply "have more faith" to fix it. Anxiety, in its most severe form, is a condition that may require professional support, whether through therapy, medication, or a combination of both. Faith and science are not in conflict here. Many people find that the combination of professional help and spiritual support is the key to overcoming anxiety. Faith can provide a solid foundation of hope and comfort, while therapy offers practical tools for managing anxiety symptoms on a day-to-day basis.

Christianity also teaches about the importance of surrender. Instead of trying to control every aspect of our lives, faith invites us to let go of that need for control and trust that God is in charge. Anxiety often arises when we feel like everything is up to us—that if we don't do everything perfectly, everything will fall apart. But the reality is that many things are out of our control. Faith reminds us that even if we do our best, the end result is not entirely in our hands. This surrender, though difficult to practice, can be deeply liberating. When we stop striving to control every detail, we experience a peace that only comes from trusting that God is in control of our lives.

One of the most common issues that causes anxiety is the fear of failure. We are afraid of not meeting the expectations of others, of failing at our goals, or of not living up to what we think we should be. The Christian faith, however, teaches us that our worth is not dependent on our performance or how successful we are in the eyes of the world. We are valuable simply because we are children of God, and that doesn't change no matter how many times we fail or how many mistakes we make. This truth can be a balm for the anxious mind that is always afraid of not being enough. When we stop measuring ourselves by the standards of the world and start seeing ourselves through the eyes of faith, we begin to let go of those fears that bind us.

Another interesting aspect is how faith invites us to change the way we view our struggles. Often, anxiety makes us feel as if every obstacle is an insurmountable threat. However, faith teaches us that challenges can be opportunities to grow, to develop our patience, our strength, and our trust in God. This change in perspective can reduce the power that anxiety has over us. Instead of seeing every difficulty as a reason to worry, we can begin to see them as part of a growth process, a test that, although difficult, has a purpose in our personal and spiritual development.

Furthermore, faith also teaches us about the value of hope. Anxiety often robs us of hope, making us feel like things will never improve, that we are stuck in a cycle of endless worry. But faith offers us a broader view. It reminds us that even when we are going through dark times, there is always light at the end of the tunnel. Hope in God gives us the strength to keep going, even when we can't see an immediate solution. This hope is not wishful thinking, but a deep conviction that God has a purpose for our lives, and that in the end, everything will work out for our good, even if we cannot currently understand how.

In conclusion, faith can be an anchor in the storm of anxiety. It invites us to trust in God rather than be consumed by our worries, to let go of the need for control, and to rest in the certainty that we are not alone in our struggles. Prayer, Christian community, and hope for a better future are valuable resources that help us find peace in the midst of chaos. Although anxiety is a reality for many, faith offers us tools to face it with courage, confidence, and serenity, reminding us that, in the end, God is always by our side.

Religious Manipulation

Religious manipulation is a phenomenon that has existed throughout history and occurs when religious beliefs are used as a tool to influence, control or exploit people. Over time, some religious institutions and leaders have found in faith a way to exert power over the masses, using fear, guilt and the promise of eternal salvation to subdue the will of believers. This type of manipulation not only has a profound impact on the minds and emotions of the faithful, but can also distort the true purpose of spirituality, which is to guide people towards a life of peace, love and understanding.

Religion, at its core, is meant to connect humans to the divine, to offer comfort in times of trouble, and to provide a sense of purpose and meaning in life. However, when used for manipulative purposes, it can become a dangerous tool. Religious manipulation occurs when people's beliefs are used to gain power, money, or influence, and in many cases, those who fall into this trap do so because they blindly trust leaders who supposedly represent God.

One of the most common methods of religious manipulation is the use of fear. From fear of divine punishment to fear of eternal damnation, the idea that one must blindly obey in order to avoid a terrible fate has been used to control people. Some religious leaders preach the idea that any doubt, questioning, or deviation from established teachings will result in divine punishment. This fear takes root deep in the minds of believers, leading them to conform and follow instructions without question. Fear is one of the most powerful emotions a human can feel, and when used in a religious context, it can lead people to act against their own best interests or even their personal morality.

Another commonly used manipulative tactic is guilt. Religious institutions often emphasize the concept of sin and human imperfection, which is not in itself negative, as the recognition of our mistakes is fundamental to spiritual growth. However, when this message is taken to the extreme, it can become a constant source of guilt and shame. Some religious teachings place such a heavy burden on individuals that the faithful may feel perpetually guilty for not living up to the ideals of perfection imposed upon them. This sense of constant guilt can be exploited by those in power to keep people under their control, offering them salvation or forgiveness only if they faithfully follow their directives.

A third method of religious manipulation is the exploitation of hope. Religion offers hope, and that is a positive thing. But some religious leaders manipulate that hope, promising material or spiritual rewards in exchange for obedience, donations, or specific actions. For example, believers are told that if they donate large sums of money to the church, they will receive financial blessings or miracles in their personal lives. This exploits the vulnerability of those who are desperate to improve their situation, making them believe that the only way to obtain relief is through blind obedience or personal sacrifice.

Furthermore, religious manipulation manifests itself in the control of information. In many religious settings, believers are discouraged from questioning or doing their own research. They are told that they must accept teachings as they are, without doubting or seeking other perspectives. This suppression of critical thinking can lead to complete dependence on religious leaders, who control what believers should believe and how they should act. By limiting access to outside information or even encouraging personal reflection, an atmosphere is created where the leader has the final say on everything from morality to personal decisions.

Another aspect of religious manipulation is the use of social exclusion. Many religious communities preach that those who do not follow their path or deviate from their teachings will be excluded, not only from the faith community, but also from eternal life. This can create a deep fear of being rejected not only by God, but also by friends and family who are part of the same religious community. The idea of being ostracized or excluded can be powerful enough to cause people to conform to teachings or practices they do not agree with, simply to avoid the pain of being rejected.

In some cases, religious manipulation can take a more active form of exploitation. This is particularly evident in situations where religious leaders abuse their power to exploit their followers emotionally, financially, or even physically. Sadly, there are documented cases where the trust of the faithful has been abused, justifying heinous acts with the idea that they are "God's will" or that the leader has a special connection to the divine that grants him the authority to act in inhumane ways. People, convinced that their faith is at stake, submit to these abuses, believing that they must do so in order to be in God's good graces.

Not all religious manipulation is so extreme, however. In many cases, manipulation comes in subtle ways, disguised as spiritual teaching or moral guidance. Faithful people may not realize they are being manipulated, as they trust that those guiding them have their spiritual well-being in mind. It is only over time, when they begin to question inconsistencies or abuses of power, that some realize they have been the subject of manipulation.

The impact of religious manipulation on individuals' mental health can be devastating. People who have been manipulated in this way often experience anxiety, depression, feelings of guilt and shame, and a profound loss of self-esteem. Furthermore, when they finally realize that they have been manipulated, they may feel betrayed not only by religious leaders, but also by religion itself, which can lead to a spiritual and emotional crisis. The recovery process can be long and painful, as it involves not only healing emotional wounds, but also rebuilding a healthy relationship with spirituality and faith.

In conclusion, religious manipulation is a misuse of faith and can have serious consequences for those who suffer from it. Although religion, in its very essence, is meant to provide peace, comfort and a connection to the divine, when it is used to control and exploit, it becomes a dangerous tool. It is essential that the faithful develop a sense of critical awareness, question the teachings they are given and ensure that their relationship with faith is one of personal and spiritual growth, and not control or blind submission. True faith should liberate, not enslave, and should empower people to live lives full of purpose, peace and love, not keep them under the yoke of manipulation.

The Concept of God and the Collective Unconscious

The concept of God has been one of the most influential ideas in human history. For millions of people around the world, God is a central force that gives meaning to life, explains the origin of everything that exists, and guides human actions. However, when we analyze this concept from a psychological perspective, it is possible to see that the idea of God is deeply intertwined with what psychologist Carl Jung called the collective unconscious. This theory holds that the human mind shares a series of ideas, symbols, and archetypes that exist beyond individual experience. The concept of God, under this perspective, would not only be a personal belief, but a manifestation of something deeper and universal that resides in the unconscious of all human beings.

The collective unconscious is a set of images and symbols that we all share, regardless of our culture or personal experiences. According to Jung, these symbols are expressed through the myths, dreams, and religions of different peoples. Although cultures may have different ways of depicting God, many share common elements: a supreme, omniscient, omnipotent being who is the source of life and spiritual guide. This suggests that the idea of a higher power is a psychological need shared by all of humanity. It is not just an invention of a specific culture, but something that has been present in all civilizations and has manifested itself in various ways throughout history.

One of the reasons the concept of God resonates so much with the human mind is because it answers fundamental questions we all ask ourselves at some point in our lives: Where did we come from? Why are we here? What is the meaning of life? Religion offers answers to these questions, and it does so in a way that satisfies both our rational minds and our deepest emotions. The collective unconscious, according to Jung, is filled with archetypes that represent these primordial ideas, and God is said to be one of the most powerful archetypes, symbolizing wholeness, perfection, and purpose.

When we look at the world's different religions, we can see how the figure of God varies, but also how there are striking similarities between cultures that, in theory, had no contact with each other. For example, in many ancient religions, God is represented as a father figure, a protective being who guides his human children and provides them with laws to live by. This image of God as father reflects a very deep archetype that we all share: the figure of the protector, the guide, the benevolent authority who looks after us. Similarly, the notion of a divine creator who gives rise to all things appears in numerous cultures, from Greek myths to Christian scriptures, through to the indigenous beliefs of America and Africa. This archetype of the "creator" is also present in the collective unconscious, manifesting itself in different ways depending on the culture, but always fulfilling the function of giving a sense of origin and purpose to human existence.

The concept of God not only answers existential questions, but also provides a framework for morality and ethics. Many religions present God as a figure who not only created the universe, but also established the rules that human beings must follow in order to live properly. This is where the collective unconscious also plays an important role. Humans, throughout history, have felt the need to live according to certain ethical and moral principles, and many times these principles have been attributed to a divine source. The fact that different cultures, with different concepts of God, share similar ethical principles (such as respect for life, justice, honesty) suggests that these values are deeply rooted in the human psyche, beyond any specific religious teaching.

The collective unconscious also explains why many people experience God in personal ways, through dreams, visions, or mystical experiences. These experiences, while varying from person to person, often have common elements that can be traced back to archetypes in the collective unconscious. For example, visions of light, feelings of deep peace, or the perception of a divine presence are experiences reported by people from different cultures and religions, and all point to something that transcends individual conscious experience. In these moments, the individual is not only experiencing a connection with something external, but also with a deep part of themselves, with an archetype that resides in their own unconscious.

It is important to note that from a psychological perspective, this does not mean that God does not exist or that He is simply a creation of the human mind. Rather, psychology suggests that the concept of God and experiences related to the divine are deeply rooted in human nature, in the very structure of our psyche. The fact that God appears in so many different forms throughout history and in so many different cultures could be interpreted as proof that there is something in the human being that always seeks that connection with the transcendental, with the divine, with something that goes beyond everyday life.

The collective unconscious, being filled with these archetypes, may also explain why religions have such power to unite people. Belief in a common God, in a divine source that we all share, creates a sense of community and belonging. Religious ceremonies, rituals, and prayers are ways for people to connect not only with God, but also with each other, on a deep, archetypal level. These practices reinforce the idea that we are all united by something greater than ourselves, something that resides both within us and outside of us.

The concept of God can also act as a psychological refuge in times of crisis. When people face difficult or traumatic situations, belief in a supreme being can provide comfort and hope. This function of God as comforter and protector is directly related to the archetypes of the collective unconscious. In times of despair, people look within for that archetypal figure to give them strength and direction. Whether they call it God, the divine light, or some other name, what they are doing is connecting with a deep part of their psyche that helps them cope.

Finally, the concept of God also influences how people view the world and themselves. For many, belief in God involves believing in a greater purpose, a divine destiny, a plan that gives meaning to all things. This belief can provide a strong sense of identity and purpose, something that is also deeply rooted in the collective unconscious. The search for purpose, for meaning in life, is one of the most powerful forces that drives human beings, and the concept of God has been one of the most universal and enduring responses to this need. By believing in a God who has a plan for us, we feel part of something greater, something that gives us direction and meaning.

In conclusion, the concept of God is intrinsically linked to the collective unconscious. Throughout history, it has been one of the most powerful and persistent ideas in the human psyche, providing answers to the deepest questions about life, purpose, and morality. Although religions may differ in their depictions of God, they all share common archetypes that reside deep within our minds. These archetypes not only shape our understanding of the divine, but also influence how we live our lives, how we relate to others, and how we deal with the challenges of existence.

Faith as a Psychological Refuge

Faith, for many people, is much more than just a belief in something greater. In times of difficulty, confusion, or pain, faith becomes a psychological refuge, an inner space where people can find comfort, strength, and meaning. It is as if, in the midst of an emotional storm, faith offers a safe place, a harbor where we can rest until the bad weather passes. To understand how this refuge works, it is important to view faith from a psychological perspective, that is, how it directly affects our minds and emotions at the times when we need it most.

When someone is facing a crisis, whether it be an illness, the loss of a loved one, financial problems, or any other hardship, it is common for them to experience a great deal of stress. This stress can manifest itself in many ways: anxiety, hopelessness, feelings of disorientation, or even depression. In such moments, the mind searches for something to hold on to, something that will give it stability when everything around it seems to be out of control. That is where faith comes into play. Believing in something greater, in a higher power that has a plan or that offers protection, allows a person to feel that they are not alone, that there is a force that gives meaning to what they are experiencing, even if they cannot fully understand it at the moment.

This psychological refuge that faith offers can be seen in many people who, facing extremely difficult circumstances, seem to find a peace that others cannot. It is not that these people do not feel fear or pain, but that, through their faith, they manage to find a way to cope. Faith gives them a different perspective. Instead of seeing their problems as something without solution or meaningless, they see them as part of a larger process, something that, at some point, will have a reason or a purpose. This perspective can greatly reduce anxiety and stress, as it transforms the way in which life's challenges are perceived.

An interesting aspect of faith is that, although it is often related to religion, it doesn't necessarily have to be. Faith, in a broader sense, is the belief in something that cannot be seen or proven, but that feels real deep within. For some, that belief is centered on God or a specific deity, while for others, faith may be in destiny, the universe, or even human potential. The important thing is that faith creates a mental framework into which people can place their fears and worries, trusting that somehow everything will be okay.

This psychological refuge that faith offers also has a basis in how our minds work. Humans have a deep need to find meaning in our lives and in the experiences we live. When something has no explanation or seems unfair, our minds can enter a state of chaos, searching for answers that are not always at hand. Faith, in this context, offers a solution. Instead of trying to understand everything logically, faith allows us to accept that there are things we simply cannot understand at that moment. This act of acceptance can be tremendously liberating, as it takes away the weight of having to solve all of life's mysteries on our own.

Furthermore, faith can also be a source of emotional strength. Instead of feeling overwhelmed by grief or uncertainty, someone who has faith can feel like they have an inexhaustible source of energy to draw on. This strength doesn't necessarily have to come from a change in external circumstances, but rather from a change in internal attitude. Believing that there is something bigger looking out for you, or that difficulties are part of a greater plan, can completely change the way you deal with adversity. This change in attitude can be what allows a person to keep going when all seems lost.

On the other hand, the psychological refuge that faith offers also has a social component. Many people find support and comfort in their faith communities. In times of difficulty, these communities offer not only a space where pain and confusion can be expressed, but also a place where emotional support can be received from others who share the same beliefs. The sense of belonging, of being surrounded by people who understand and share the same worldview, can be a key factor in emotional recovery. Feeling that one is not alone, that there are others who also believe and who have gone through similar experiences, reinforces the refuge that faith provides.

The power of faith as a refuge can also be seen in how it helps people cope with fear of the unknown, especially in matters such as death or suffering. The uncertainty of what happens after life, or why bad things happen, can be terrifying. However, faith provides answers, or at least a sense of peace, in the face of such questions. Believing that there is something after death, or that suffering has a greater purpose, can ease fear and offer a kind of reassurance in the face of the inevitable.

The power of faith in times of despair cannot be underestimated. When all else seems to fail, when logical solutions no longer suffice, faith can be the last resort a person clings to. And often, it is precisely that last resort that allows them to pull through. The human mind has an incredible capacity for adaptation, and faith is one of the most powerful tools it has for finding meaning in even the darkest of circumstances.

Of course, not everyone finds refuge in faith in the same way. Some people may have difficulty believing, especially when faced with very painful situations. For these people, the idea of trusting in something they cannot see or understand may seem impossible. Even in these cases, however, faith can be a useful tool if it is seen as a way of letting go of control. Sometimes the simple act of letting go of resisting what is happening, of accepting that you are not in control of everything, can offer a kind of psychological refuge.

In short, faith functions as a psychological refuge because it offers a way to face pain, fear, and uncertainty from a different perspective. It allows us to let go of control, accept that not everything is in our hands, and trust that somehow everything will work out. Whether through belief in God, fate, or human potential, faith provides a mental and emotional space where people can find comfort, strength, and meaning. In the darkest of times, it is this refuge that often makes the difference between giving up or moving forward.

Religion and the Fear of Punishment

Religion has played a crucial role in people's lives since ancient times, shaping their beliefs, behaviors, and values. One of the most powerful ways religion has influenced human minds is through the fear of punishment. This fear has been used as a means to regulate behavior, setting clear boundaries on what is considered right and wrong. From a psychological standpoint, the fear of punishment is a very effective mechanism to keep people within a certain framework of behavior, since no one wants to suffer the consequences of going against the rules they have been taught since childhood.

In many religions, particularly Christianity, it has been taught that there is a divine punishment for those who do not follow the rules imposed by God. This punishment is often depicted as hell, a place of eternal torment where souls are sent after death if they have not lived according to religious precepts. The idea of hell is extremely terrifying, as it is not a simple temporary punishment, but something eternal and completely irreversible. This has led many people to live in constant fear of making mistakes, disobeying the rules, and even thinking incorrectly, because they feel that any deviation could lead them to that terrible fate.

This fear of punishment not only affects people's external behavior, but also their emotional state. Many times, the fear of being punished by God generates high levels of anxiety, especially in those who feel unable to meet religious expectations. Religion, in this context, not only sets rules of conduct, but also gets into people's innermost thoughts and desires. For example, in Christianity it is taught that even impure thoughts can be grounds for punishment. This creates very great psychological pressure, since it is not only about what one does, but also about what one thinks. This internal control imposed by the fear of punishment can make people feel guilty and anxious even when they have done nothing wrong, but have had thoughts that they consider "sinful."

Another way in which fear of punishment manifests itself in religion is through rules about sin. Religions often clearly define what they consider to be sinful – that is, what goes against God's will. Sins are classified in various ways, but what is common to almost all religions is the idea that sin must be punished. This punishment can manifest itself in different ways – from consequences in earthly life, such as misfortune, illness or suffering, to punishments in the afterlife. This creates a strong incentive for people to follow religious rules, not only out of a desire to do the right thing, but out of fear of what might happen to them if they don't.

Fear of punishment also affects people's decisions. For example, someone who is considering doing something that they know is religiously wrong may decide not to do it simply because they are afraid of the consequences. This fear acts as a psychological barrier that prevents certain actions from being carried out, even though they might seem beneficial or desirable at the time. This can have a positive effect in some cases, as it helps to avoid destructive or harmful behavior. However, it can also have a negative effect, as it can prevent people from making decisions based on their own judgment and conscience, and instead act solely out of fear.

It is important to understand that fear of punishment is not only about fear of divine consequences after death. Many religions teach that God punishes in this life as well. This can include illness, accidents, financial loss, or any type of suffering. This belief can lead people to view anything bad that happens to them as a punishment for something they did wrong. If a person becomes seriously ill or loses their job, they may think they are being punished for not following religious precepts properly. This type of belief can increase the person's emotional burden, as they are not only facing a difficult situation, but they also feel that it is their fault and that God is punishing them.

From a psychological standpoint, fear of religious punishment can create a cycle of guilt and fear that is difficult to break. People who constantly fear doing something wrong and being punished often live in a state of emotional tension. Every decision, every thought, every action becomes a potential source of guilt, which increases stress and anxiety. In many cases, this fear can lead to compulsive behaviors, such as the need to constantly pray or perform religious rituals to make sure they are on the "right path." Although these behaviors may offer temporary relief, the underlying fear is still there, and people may feel that they are never quite sure that they have avoided punishment.

Fear of punishment has also historically been used as a tool of social control. Many religious institutions have leveraged this fear to keep the masses under control. By instilling the fear that any disobedience or disregard for religious norms will be punished severely, religious authorities have succeeded in getting people to faithfully follow the rules, even when these rules are not always fair or reasonable. This type of fear manipulation has allowed religious institutions to maintain their power and influence over large groups of people for centuries. Even today, in some places, fear of divine punishment remains a powerful tool to keep people aligned with the values and norms of the dominant religion.

It is interesting to note how fear of punishment also affects interpersonal relationships within religious communities. In many religious cultures, people monitor the behavior of others and are on the lookout for any transgressions. This type of social surveillance can create an atmosphere of distrust, where people fear not only being punished by God, but also by their community. Being judged or rejected by other believers can be seen as a form of punishment in itself, which adds an extra layer of pressure to conform to religious norms.

Despite the negative aspects that fear of punishment can have, it is important to note that for many people, this fear has also served as a form of moral discipline. The fear of being punished can lead people to behave more ethically and compassionately.

However, this behavior is based on fear, and not on a genuine desire to do good. This raises an important question: Is it better to act rightly out of fear of punishment or out of an internal sense of what is just and right?

In conclusion, the fear of punishment is one of the most powerful forces that religion has used to influence human minds. This fear affects not only external behavior, but also the emotional and psychological state of people. From the threat of hell to the idea that any misfortune in life is a divine punishment, the fear of punishment has shaped the way people view the world, themselves, and others. Although this fear can have positive effects in maintaining moral behavior, it can also create an emotional and psychological burden that is difficult to bear.

Religion and Self-esteem

Religion and self-esteem are two aspects of life that, although they may seem separate, are deeply connected in many people's experience. Religion, by offering a framework of beliefs, norms, and values, can significantly influence how we perceive ourselves and how we value our actions and our place in the world. Self-esteem, which is how we evaluate our own worth and ability, can be affected both positively and negatively by the influence of religious beliefs.

For some people, religion can be a source of self-esteem and personal confidence. When a person feels that they are living according to the tenets of their faith, they may experience a sense of pride and personal satisfaction. Following the teachings of a religion and meeting its expectations can make a person feel valued, loved, and accepted, both by God and by their religious community. This type of external recognition, combined with an internal belief that one is living rightly, can be a great source of self-esteem. In this sense, religion can provide clear guidance on how to be a "good person," which reinforces a positive sense of self.

On the other hand, when people feel that they do not meet the high standards imposed by their religion, religion can become a source of low self-esteem. Many religions teach that human beings are inherently imperfect or sinful and that they need to constantly strive to attain salvation or divine grace. This belief can create a feeling of inadequacy in some people, who see themselves as incapable of meeting religious standards. The constant emphasis on sin and the need for redemption can lead people to see themselves as flawed or unworthy, which directly impacts their self-esteem.

One of the problems that many people face in their relationship between religion and self-esteem is the feeling that they are never good enough. This can occur in religions that have strict standards about what is considered moral behavior. For example, in some branches of Christianity, people are expected to be humble, pious, generous, and always attentive to the needs of others. Although these are important values, they can create excessive pressure on some people, who feel that they are not capable of always living up to these ideals. The fear of not being good enough in the eyes of God or their religious community can lead to a strong feeling of inadequacy and severely affect self-esteem.

It is important to recognize that in many religions, it is taught that self-esteem should not come from personal achievements or external recognition, but from one's relationship with God. In this context, self-esteem is based on the fact that a person is loved and valued by God, regardless of their flaws or failures. This idea can be incredibly liberating for some people, as it allows them to feel that their worth is not dependent on what they do, but on who they are at their core as beings created by God. This form of faith-based self-esteem can be very powerful, especially in times of doubt or difficulty, as it offers a sense of intrinsic worth that is not dependent on external circumstances.

However, this same belief can also have a dark side. In some religions, it is taught that a person's worth is completely subordinate to the will of God and that without divine grace, a person has no value in and of themselves. This idea can lead some people to believe that they have no intrinsic value apart from their relationship with God, which can make them feel dependent on divine approval in order to feel valuable. If these people experience a crisis of faith or feel that they have failed in their relationship with God, their self-esteem can plummet, as their personal worth is completely tied to their compliance with religious precepts.

Another interesting aspect of the relationship between religion and self-esteem is how religious community can influence a person's sense of self-worth. In many religions, community is a key pillar. Membership of a religious group can offer a strong sense of identity and belonging, which can improve self-esteem. When a person feels accepted and valued by their religious community, they may develop a more positive sense of self. Community can provide emotional support, guidance, and a space where people feel heard and understood, which is key to healthy self-esteem.

However, the opposite can also happen. In some religious communities, standards and expectations can be so strict that people feel like they are constantly under judgment. Criticism or rejection from a religious community can be devastating to a person's self-esteem, as they may interpret it as a sign that they are not good enough in the eyes of God or their fellow believers. Instead of feeling supported and valued, these people may feel isolated, rejected, or unworthy, which negatively affects their self-esteem.

Additionally, it is important to consider how religious teachings about forgiveness and grace can affect self-esteem. In many religions, it is taught that although human beings are imperfect, there is always an opportunity to redeem oneself and be forgiven. This idea can be a source of hope and healing for people who struggle with low self-esteem, as it offers them the possibility of a new beginning and of being accepted despite their failings. Divine forgiveness can be seen as a way to restore self-esteem, as it allows people to free themselves from the weight of guilt and shame.

However, some people may have difficulty accepting the concept of forgiveness, which affects their self-esteem. If a person believes that their sins or mistakes are too great to be forgiven, or if they feel that they are not worthy of forgiveness, they may become trapped in a cycle of self-judgment and blame. This inability to accept forgiveness, both from themselves and from God, can perpetuate low self-esteem and make it difficult to develop a positive self-image.

Finally, it is essential to highlight how religious teachings on humility can interact with self-esteem. Many religions promote the idea that it is important to be humble and not seek self-exaltation. Although humility is an important value, it can be misinterpreted by some people, who believe that being humble means devaluing oneself or failing to recognize one's own qualities and achievements. This misinterpretation of humility can lead some people to suppress their self-esteem, believing that they must minimize their worth in order to please God or their religious community.

In conclusion, the relationship between religion and self-esteem is complex and multifaceted. Religion can be a powerful source of self-esteem for those who feel aligned with its beliefs and values, providing them with a sense of purpose, belonging, and intrinsic worth. However, it can also be a source of internal conflict for those who struggle with religious expectations or the feeling that they are never good enough. The key to developing healthy self-esteem in the religious context lies in finding a balance between humility and recognition of one's own worth, and in learning to accept both one's own flaws and the grace and forgiveness that religion can offer.

The Psychological Impact of Religious Leadership

Religious leadership has a profound impact on the lives of people who are part of faith communities. This type of leadership, which can be exercised by pastors, priests, ministers or any figure representing authority within a religion, not only influences the religious practice of believers, but also their psychological well-being. For many, the religious leader becomes a guiding figure in both the spiritual and personal realms, helping people deal with everyday problems, existential doubts, and difficult emotional situations. However, this influence can be both positive and negative, depending on the quality of the leadership and the relationship built with the members of the community.

On the positive side, a religious leader can act as a mentor who offers comfort, support, and guidance. This type of leader can provide a sense of emotional and psychological stability in times of crisis, reminding people that they are not alone and can always count on their faith community. The feeling of belonging to a group, where a leader provides security and direction, can be incredibly beneficial to mental health. For example, in times of grief, anxiety, or depression, a person may turn to their religious leader for words of encouragement to help them view life from a perspective of hope and confidence that things will get better.

A good religious leader not only teaches about faith, but also shows compassion and empathy. This emotional connection with followers is essential to fostering an environment of support and personal growth. Many people look to their leaders for role models, and when the leader is a kind, fair, and approachable figure, they can inspire others to improve their own lives. Psychologically, this can help people feel a greater sense of purpose and direction, which contributes to better mental health. Additionally, religious leadership can foster resilience, helping people find strength in their faith during difficult times.

On the other hand, when religious leadership is exercised in an authoritarian or manipulative manner, the psychological impact can be devastating. Some people may feel controlled or pressured by leaders who use their authority to impose strict rules or create an environment of fear. This type of leadership does not promote mental well-being, but instead generates distress and feelings of guilt. When religious leaders resort to fear or guilt to maintain control over their followers, many people experience low self-esteem and a constant fear of judgment, both from God and from the community. This can lead to a cycle of anxiety and self-criticism that severely affects mental health.

Furthermore, some religious leaders may take advantage of their position to emotionally manipulate people, leading them to believe that they must blindly follow their instructions without question. This can create psychological dependency, where people do not feel capable of making important decisions for themselves without first consulting their religious leader. This loss of autonomy can be harmful, as it can hinder personal development and the ability to deal with life's challenges independently.

Rather than empowering people, this type of leadership weakens them psychologically.

Another aspect of religious leadership that can have a significant impact on people's psychology is how expectations are managed within the community. A religious leader who demands unattainable perfection from his or her followers can cause deep psychological damage. Some people may feel constantly judged or inadequate, struggling to meet expectations that are impossible to achieve. This type of environment can lead to increased anxiety, depression, and feelings of failure. Instead of feeling supported and understood, these people may experience emotional isolation and a sense that they are never good enough for their community or for God.

However, not all authoritarian or strict religious leadership has a negative impact. In some cases, people seek out leaders who offer clear and firm rules, as this provides a sense of security and structure in their lives. For some people, having a leader tell them exactly what to do can be comforting, as it takes away the responsibility of making difficult decisions on their own. Although this dependent relationship may not be ideal for long-term personal development, it can offer short-term relief for those who feel overwhelmed by life's uncertainties.

It is important to note that the psychological impact of religious leadership can also vary depending on the cultural and social context. In some cultures, the religious leader occupies a central role in community life, and his or her influence can extend to all areas of a person's life, from family relationships to career decisions. In these cases, the religious leader not only guides in matters of faith, but also dictates social and ethical norms that community members must follow. In these situations, the psychological influence of religious leadership is even more profound, affecting almost every aspect of people's identity and daily lives.

When religious leadership is combined with political power, its psychological impact can become even more complicated. In some contexts, religious leaders have a direct influence over the laws and policies of a country or region, meaning that their authority not only affects people's spiritual lives, but also their public lives. This type of leadership can reinforce a sense of social conformity, where people feel they must follow religious teachings in order to be accepted both in their community and in society at large. This can lead to additional psychological pressure, as people not only feel responsible to God, but also to the social system in which they live.

On the other hand, religious leadership can be a powerful force for social and psychological change. Many religious leaders have been catalysts for social justice and human rights movements, using their position of influence to promote people's well-being and dignity. In these cases, the psychological impact of religious leadership can be enormously positive, helping to empower people and motivate them to strive for a better world. A religious leader who is committed to the well-being of his or her followers can inspire a sense of hope and purpose that transforms lives and communities.

Ultimately, the psychological impact of religious leadership depends largely on the leadership style and the relationship established between the leader and his or her followers. Leadership based on love, compassion, and respect can be an incredibly powerful source of psychological well-being. However, when leadership is exercised in an oppressive or manipulative manner, it can cause significant damage to mental health. For this reason, it is crucial for religious leaders to be aware of the responsibility they have for the emotional and psychological lives of the people they lead, and to use their influence to promote well-being rather than to control or manipulate.

For followers, it is important to recognize that while religious leaders can offer valuable guidance, psychological well-being and mental health ultimately depend on each person's ability to make decisions for themselves, build healthy relationships, and find a balance between faith and personal autonomy.

The Psychology of Religious Conversion

Religious conversion is one of the most fascinating phenomena in the field of psychology, as it involves a profound change not only in a person's beliefs, but also in their identity, their way of seeing the world, and how they relate to others. When someone experiences a conversion, whether to a new religion or a deeper reaffirmation of their existing faith, the psychological effects can be intense and life-changing. Religious conversion can occur in many ways, but it always involves a number of psychological factors that help to understand why someone chooses, or feels the need to, change their spiritual belief.

One of the first things to consider when we talk about religious conversion is the emotional state of the person before the conversion. In many cases, people who convert are going through a personal crisis or a period of uncertainty in their lives. This crisis can be emotional, such as the loss of a loved one, a breakup, or a feeling of existential emptiness. Or it can be a more practical crisis, such as financial problems, work or family difficulties. During these times, people often look for something that will provide them with stability, comfort, and a new way of understanding their situation. Religion, for many, offers answers and a sense of purpose that can help overcome these difficulties.

Psychology explains that in these times of vulnerability, the mind is more open to new ideas and beliefs. This does not mean that religious conversion only occurs in times of weakness, but it does mean that people in situations of stress or uncertainty are more likely to seek refuge in something that offers them security. Religion, with its promises of salvation, spiritual comfort, and a supportive community, seems like an ideal solution. The conversion process often begins with an initial contact with religion or a religious community, which may be through a friend, family member, a spiritual experience, or even simply attending a church or place of worship.

Once a person comes into contact with this new belief, a psychological phenomenon called cognitive dissonance occurs. This concept refers to the discomfort we feel when our current beliefs or values conflict with new information or experience. In the case of religious conversion, the person may experience a sense of mismatch between his or her current life and the promise of a fuller or more meaningful life offered by the new religion. This dissonance creates an internal pressure to resolve the conflict, and the way in which it is resolved often leads to conversion.

Resolving this dissonance can take time. Some people begin attending religious services, reading sacred texts, or talking to other believers to better understand the new religion. As they delve deeper into the faith, the cognitive dissonance diminishes as the person begins to accept the new beliefs as a solution to their existential problems or questions. At this point, conversion becomes a gradual process in which the person begins to internalize religious teachings and apply those principles to their daily lives.

But religious conversion is not just a change of beliefs; it also involves a transformation in the person's identity. This change of identity is crucial in the psychological process of conversion. Through religion, the person not only adopts a new belief system, but also begins to see himself or herself differently. For example, he or she may begin to see himself or herself as a son or daughter of God, as someone who has a divine purpose, or as someone who has been forgiven for past mistakes. This change in identity provides a sense of renewal, which can be very powerful from a psychological perspective. The person feels that he or she has been reborn, that he or she has left behind a previous life filled with mistakes or emptiness, and that he or she now has a new life with purpose and direction.

Another important psychological factor in religious conversion is belonging to a community. Most religions not only offer a belief system, but also a community of people who share those values and beliefs. Feeling part of a community can be incredibly valuable to a person going through a conversion. This sense of belonging and acceptance can further reinforce the decision to adopt the new faith. Additionally, social interactions within the religious community can help the person feel supported, understood, and less alone in their transformation process.

It is also important to note that religious conversion can bring with it a sense of personal control. For many people, life can feel chaotic and unpredictable. Religion, with its clear teachings about right and wrong, the purpose of life, and the meaning of existence, offers structure and order that can make people feel more in control of their lives. Having answers to difficult questions or feeling that there is a greater plan can reduce anxiety and provide a sense of inner peace. Psychologically, this is very beneficial, as it reduces stress levels and increases a sense of overall well-being.

However, we must also recognize that not all religious conversions are necessarily positive. In some cases, conversion may be the result of social pressure or emotional manipulation. People who are in a state of emotional or mental vulnerability may be susceptible to external influences, and some religious communities or leaders may take advantage of this vulnerability to attract new followers. In these cases, conversion may not be based on a genuine search for faith, but on a need to belong or feel accepted, which in the long term could lead to internal conflicts if the person realizes that they have adopted beliefs that are not truly theirs.

The psychology of conversion also invites us to consider the role of intense emotional experiences. For many people, conversion is linked to a profound spiritual experience that changes the way they see the world. These experiences can be interpreted as an encounter with the divine, a revelation, or a moment of clarity. Psychologically, these experiences can be so powerful that they lead to a radical transformation in the way a person understands his or her life and purpose. These intense emotions not only reinforce the conversion, but also create an emotional connection to the new faith that is difficult to break.

In short, religious conversion is a complex process involving multiple psychological factors, from seeking solace in times of crisis, to resolving cognitive dissonance, to transforming one's identity. This process can bring peace, meaning, and belonging to people's lives, but it can also arise in contexts where social pressure or manipulation plays a role. Every conversion is unique, and understanding the psychology behind this phenomenon allows us to see more clearly why religion remains such a powerful force in people's lives. In the end, conversion is not just a change of beliefs, but a total renewal of how a person views themselves and the world around them.

Christianity and the Psychology of Self-Sacrifice

Christianity, from its very beginnings, has emphasized the importance of self-sacrifice as an act of love, faith, and self-giving. This idea of sacrificing oneself for the good of others, or for a greater cause, is one of the fundamental pillars of the Christian faith. The figure of Jesus Christ, who sacrificed himself on the cross to redeem the sins of humanity, is the ultimate example of this concept. But beyond the biblical story, self-sacrifice in Christianity has profound psychological implications, and is an important part of how many people experience their faith in everyday life.

From a psychological perspective, self-sacrifice can be seen as a way to find meaning and purpose in life. Many people, when experiencing hardship or facing challenges, can find comfort in the idea that their suffering has a greater purpose. The belief that by sacrificing themselves they are following the example of Christ or contributing to the well-being of others gives them a sense of control and direction in the midst of adversity. This sense of purpose can alleviate the stress and anxiety that often accompany difficult times.

Sacrifice is also closely related to the idea of renunciation. In Christianity, believers are encouraged to give up selfish desires, earthly pleasures, and in some cases even their own well-being, in favor of others or their relationship with God. This process of renunciation can be seen as a form of self-discipline, where the individual learns to control their impulses and desires in order to achieve a more spiritual life. Psychologically, this self-discipline can have positive effects, as it teaches the person to delay gratification, to focus on long-term goals, and to develop greater control over their emotions and actions.

However, self-sacrifice in Christianity is not just about giving up material things or temporary pleasures. Often, it involves emotional or interpersonal sacrifices. This can include forgiving someone who has wronged us, helping those in need, or even devoting time and effort to causes that do not offer immediate or tangible rewards.

These acts of sacrifice, while they may be difficult, often bring a deep sense of satisfaction and connection to something greater than oneself.

When a person makes a sacrifice for another, whether for family, friends, or even strangers, they experience an increase in self-esteem and their sense of personal worth. This occurs because sacrifice is associated with the idea of doing the right thing, being a good person, or acting according to the highest moral principles. For Christians, these principles are linked to the commandments of love and compassion taught by Jesus, reinforcing the idea that self-sacrifice is a direct expression of their faith. Psychologically, this reinforces the believer's identity and values, allowing them to feel at peace with themselves and their relationship with God.

Another important aspect of sacrifice in Christianity is its relationship to redemption. In many cases, sacrifice is seen as a way to atone for wrongs or sins committed. The idea that one can "pay" for wrongdoing or personal mistakes through sacrifice has a strong psychological component, as it provides a form of relief from guilt and remorse. When a person feels that they have done something wrong, sacrifice becomes a tangible way to right that wrong, to balance out what is wrong, and to restore a sense of moral equilibrium.

Self-sacrifice also has an impact on the Christian community. Just as Jesus sacrificed himself for humanity, believers are called to sacrifice for one another. This act of mutual sacrifice creates strong bonds between members of the community, as each is willing to put the needs of the other above his or her own. Psychologically, this sense of community and mutual support strengthens group identity, creating a network of interpersonal relationships that provides emotional and social support. In times of crisis, this sense of community can be a vital source of strength and resilience.

However, it is also important to recognize that self-sacrifice in Christianity can have a dark side when taken to the extreme. Some people may feel compelled to sacrifice so much of themselves that they neglect their own well-being, both physical and emotional. In these cases, sacrifice is no longer a healthy expression of faith, but a burden that can lead a person to self-denial and, in some cases, depression or burnout. That is why, from a psychological standpoint, it is important to find a balance between self-sacrifice and self-care. Sacrificing yourself for others should not mean destroying yourself in the process.

Sacrifice in Christianity is also linked to the concept of humility. By sacrificing something for another person, the individual places themselves in a position of service. This act of humility can be very beneficial for mental health, as it helps the person to detach from their ego and see the world from a broader perspective. Instead of focusing on their own problems or desires, the person learns to care about the well-being of others. From a psychological perspective, this can reduce anxiety and stress, as the person does not feel as caught up in their own personal problems.

Furthermore, self-sacrifice in Christianity is often accompanied by the idea of future reward. Although there may not be immediate rewards for sacrificing time, energy, or resources, the belief in a heavenly reward or eternal life in heaven provides a powerful psychological incentive. This belief can help people cope with sacrifices in the present, as they trust that these sacrifices will be rewarded in the future. This expectation of reward can make the act of sacrificing more bearable, and in some cases even pleasurable, as it reinforces the idea that suffering serves a greater purpose.

In short, self-sacrifice in Christianity is a profound concept that has multiple psychological dimensions. From alleviating suffering through a sense of purpose, to strengthening self-esteem and community connections, sacrifice plays a crucial role in how Christians experience their faith. Although there may be risks associated with excessive sacrifice, when practiced in a balanced way, it can be a source of great emotional and spiritual strength. Through sacrifice, believers not only connect more deeply with their faith, but also with others, finding deeper meaning in their lives and in their relationship with God.

Adrian Collins

The Psychology of Faith in the 21st Century

The psychology of faith in the 21st century is a complex topic that reflects how religious beliefs continue to influence the human mind, but in ways that have been transformed by social, cultural, and technological changes. In an age marked by globalization, instant access to information, and the advancement of science, faith remains a fundamental aspect of many people's lives. However, the ways in which people experience and practice their faith have evolved. Today, faith is not lived solely within traditional structures such as churches or temples, but has spread to new spaces such as social media, spiritual movements, and virtual communities. Despite these changes, the impact of faith on the human mind remains significant.

One of the main ways that faith impacts psychology in the 21st century is through a sense of belonging. In an increasingly disconnected world, where people often feel isolated despite being connected virtually, faith offers a community, a place where people can share their beliefs and values. From a psychological standpoint, belonging to a group that shares the same faith can provide emotional security, reduce stress, and offer support in times of crisis. Faith acts as a safety net, especially when people are going through hardship or times of uncertainty. Knowing that one is not alone and that one belongs to something bigger can be a powerful anchor in a world filled with chaos and uncertainty.

In the 21st century, people live in an era where science and reason play a crucial role in daily life. Despite scientific advances, many people continue to find solace in faith, as it answers questions that science cannot answer. From a psychological standpoint, faith serves a function in making sense of the unexplainable. Topics such as death, the purpose of life, or the existence of the soul are difficult to approach from a purely rational perspective. This is where faith comes into play, providing a narrative that can help people deal with these deep and often distressing topics. Psychologically, having a firm belief in something transcendent can reduce existential anxiety and offer a peace of mind that science, on its own, cannot provide.

Faith also has a psychological effect on how people deal with adversity. For many, belief in a higher power or divine purpose allows them to cope with difficult situations with more serenity. When someone believes that everything happens for a reason or that they are under the care of a divine force, they are more likely to face problems with an attitude of resilience. In the 21st century, where people are constantly facing social, economic, and personal pressures, faith acts as an internal resource that allows them to keep going. This psychological aspect of faith is deeply rooted in the way people seek to overcome daily stress and hardships. For those who have a strong belief, faith is not only a spiritual refuge, but also a psychological tool that gives them the strength to keep going.

In this century, faith has also been challenged by the plurality of beliefs and constant contact with other cultures and religions. Through the internet and social media, people are exposed to different viewpoints, which has led to greater diversity in the way faith is experienced. This phenomenon has had an interesting psychological impact: for some, this exposure to different beliefs has strengthened their faith, while for others it has led to doubts and questioning. In a globalized world, faith is no longer something that is taken for granted; it becomes a conscious choice that people must make. Psychologically, this choice can be liberating, as it allows people to explore different beliefs and find the one that resonates most with them. However, it can also be a source of distress for those who feel they must question or redefine what they previously took for granted.

Another dimension of faith in the 21st century is its relationship with technology. Churches and religious communities have begun to adapt to the digital age, offering online services, virtual prayer groups, and religious content through platforms such as YouTube, Facebook, or Instagram. From a psychological point of view, this has a double effect. On the one hand, it allows people to keep their faith active and connected to a community, even if they are physically distant or isolated. But on the other hand, it can also dilute the spiritual experience, by making the act of faith become more superficial or consumable, like any other digital content. The psychology of faith in the 21st century, then, must deal with this balance between genuine connection and technological overexposure.

A crucial issue that also needs to be addressed is the role of faith in mental health in the 21st century. More and more studies show that faith and spirituality can have a positive effect on mental health. For many people, practicing their faith helps them deal with depression, anxiety, and stress. Prayer, meditation, and other religious rituals have been used as tools to calm the mind and find emotional balance. From a psychological perspective, these acts of faith function as coping mechanisms that allow people to reduce their stress levels, feel more connected to something greater than themselves, and ultimately find comfort in difficult times.

However, one cannot ignore the fact that faith can also have negative effects on people's psychology, especially when it is used to justify control or manipulation. In some situations, religion can be used as a tool of power, where religious leaders impose their worldview and demand behavior that can be detrimental to people's psychological freedom. In the 21st century, people need to be more aware of these dangers and learn to find a healthy balance between their personal faith and their psychological well-being. Faith should be a source of strength and support, not a burden or a form of manipulation.

Finally, the psychology of faith in the 21st century also reflects a shift in the way people view their relationship with the divine. Whereas in previous centuries, faith was primarily experienced within traditional religious structures, today many people seek a more personal and individual relationship with the sacred. This more intimate approach allows people to customize their faith according to their individual needs and experiences. Psychologically, this can be very beneficial, as it allows people to feel that they have active control over their spirituality and that they can adapt it to meet their own emotional and mental needs.

In short, faith in the 21st century continues to play a central role in human psychology, but it does so in ways that have evolved over time. From a sense of belonging and relief from stress to the search for answers to existential questions, faith continues to be a refuge for millions of people. At the same time, technology, globalization, and a plurality of beliefs have transformed the way people practice and experience their faith. The psychology of faith in this century is a blend of tradition and modernity, and it remains an essential part of human life, both in its positive aspects and in its challenges.